DOGS OF
BROOKLYN

Susie DeFord

Photographs by Dennis Riley
Designed by: Claudean Wheeler
Cover illustration by radoma/Fotolia.com & hannahfelicity/Fotolia.com

Published by Dog Poet Laureate Press
Brooklyn, NY
www.dogpoetlaureate.wordpress.com
www.susiedeford.com

ISBN 13: 978-0615565712
ISBN 10: 0615565719

CONTENTS

I. THE CIRCUS IS IN TOWN

2. THE DOGS OF BROOKLYN

DOG PHOTOS BY DENNIS RILEY

"I think I could turn and live with animals,
they are so placid and self-contained
I stand and look at them long and long.
They do not sweat and whine about their condition,
They do not lie awake in the dark and weep for their sins,
They do not make me sick discussing their duty to God,
Not one is dissatisfied,
not one is demented with the mania of owning things,
Not one kneels to another,
nor to his kind that lived thousands of years ago,
Not one is respectable or industrious over the whole earth."

—WALT WHITMAN

1.
THE CIRCUS
IS IN
TOWN

PROSPECT HEIGHTS POP

Walking home from the Q train, dogs and coffee
shops split street strut, brownstone buildings
and big trees bud, shooting up from the sidewalk,

dreadlocked drug dealers stalk, hanging on changing
corners—the neighborhood watch while Maclaren
Mafia mommies' doublewide strollers scream on by.

Sidewalk block, I weave and wave through the window
at big, soft Audrey working in the new chi-chi bakery.
Better than the lemon cookies, she always says hello

and remembers my coffee. Soul tracks for sale outside
the Key Food serenade as macho men swallow me
with their scary smiles. The tough Brooklyn guys

at Acme Pet Shop on Vanderbilt Avenue with their old
orange cat Knuckles chuckle at their Akita pup Lefty
as he jumps up to box me. Head down Prospect past

Harry and three-legged Fred lounging, hogging up
the sidewalk looking for strokes and extra treats
to make up for his hop-walk like a bouncing spring.

Hit Underhill and follow the Jah Love guy with his
giant boombox blasting reggae, doing his slow strange
walking meditation, "Jesus Loves You" sign strapped

to his back, and I think he must have, to have given
me this neighborhood so suited to the swing dance
bopping in my big band mind. Click the vestibule keys,

check the mail, doors squeal and slam like a drumbeat.
I dance up the dirty, dark stairs to the tiny shoebox
apartment where Itty Pity, hearing me wrestle the locks,

starts howling her blues: *My mama been gone, left me
all alone. Said my mama been gone, left me all alone.
She run around with them dogs, to keep the lights on.*

OLD MAN OF STERLING PLACE

The cats hanging in the windowsills on Sterling Place
arch their backs when the dogs and I pass by. I wave
at Zigzag barking madly from the window. He raves,
little Bella's got him trapped up on the bed, her chase
and growl intimidating only him. The soft white face
of Winston Bunny Biallystock III begs a Rapunzel save
from his 3rd floor tower across the way. He behaves
better than the old man at number 442, a grouch crazed
leaning over his broom and cane. Smashed down from
carrying his anger anchor grumbling, he teeters on bow
legs that look about to snap off sideways. Mistake made,
threw our waste in his can, he launches the poop-bag-bomb
back at us from behind. It hits the door hard; heart hollow
I drag the dogs inside realizing I'd taken on his weight.

DEATH OF A LOVE JUNKIE
For Dela

Lightning crack thunder hunger rumble stomach
quease. The banks of the Delaware River heave
    water, freezing rain, sleet. Storm-shivering

angel descends covered in thick-stick brown wire.
Big triangle ears heavy with hearing, big sad mud
    puddle eyes seeking safety within the trees

and arms of a couple of campers trying to keep warm.
They brought you back to Brooklyn with a bellyful
    of pups. I met you on a bustling block,

you were seeking strokes for your swollen frame,
a love junkie, a poet-sniffing dog here to save us
    from our heads full of words and lives

lacking reason. Then Tana came, your golden girl,
your pup that never grew up, just like the little girl
    I am groaning in this grown up body, going

gray, dry, and wrinkly. You nursed us all, licking
scars to heal, ours and your own. My miscarriage
    mourning-morning in purgatory park-bound,

me moping, you mischievously barking, chastising
loud garbage trucks along the way. Park reached,
    lost leash leap, you chased darts of yellow,

gray, green. Carried away, you crashed backs of knees
sweeping ladies off their feet. They weren't happy.
    Moved to the country, back to the storm shake.

Pursuing porcupines, coming home looking like a tribal
elder, a shaman, a medicine-woman-witch, quills piercing
    septum, lips, cheek. Black magic bumps grew

in your breast—no reprieve. From my own sickness
you were a pilgrimage, a Yatra, a retreat. I traveled
    to see you one last time. Lost in the lush

Catskill woods on the way and I stared out the window
and pretended to enjoy the scenery. When I arrived
    you wouldn't look at me. You just sat real close,

slower than before until your river dried up. Malignant
memory, heat out in this city, morning empty playground
    snow glow playing powder tracks clear to the dead

grass buried below. I swear, you and the other dogs
of Brooklyn were sent to save me from all these lonely
    days in the autumn heat and trash confetti streets.

A THOUSAND SPARROWS

The snow has been replaced with white petals falling
from the apple blossom trees. Hard green buds
breaking out of thawing limbs extending to the sun.

A thousand sparrows scream, hatched and hungry,
soon to be kicked out of the nest. Some of them
won't make it, the dogs sniff out their featherless,

naked pink bodies scattered on the sidewalk to eat.
I won't allow it, make mulched tree stumps instant
cemeteries. The kids from Little League parade down

7th Avenue, hoodlums wielding bats in their matching
yellow caps while in the distance ritual drums beat.
In Prospect Park people start shedding coats and clothes,

lounging in lumps in the big field, pale skin blinding
everyone. While the apartment buildings peer down
from above at their shaded flowers fighting to bloom.

We all try to suck in the sun like oxygen after months
of cold gray hibernating. I claw at my eyes and sneeze,
my body fighting even the seasons changing. Rain relief,

pollen drowning, the dogs and I trudge through fat drops
falling. Sally shakes and sulks while Eva stink-eyes me
for making them walk wet. We'd all rather stay cozy

in our tiny apartments instead of be slicked shower sick.
We dance a duck and dodge beneath splintered old building
awnings and stare at the sky waiting for the rain to run out.

MAKING PEACE WITH THE FLOWERS

Sneezing at the pollen beauty of spring,
    I want to move
away from the flowers so I won't want
       them anymore.
They call to me and tease—with no pruning
    I'm afraid someday
they'll overtake me. So I run to cement
       gardens, buildings
bloom wildly into the sky, and this is
       beautiful to me.
The gardeners with their hard
       hats and dirty jeans
tame the wildness of the city lit in
       traffic light winks.
But even here the flowers still find me.
       They mock me,
pink in their plastic sacks on street corners,
    cunningly they find
their way into my tea. Chamomile, you are
       the most exquisite
flower. I adore the charm of your pale
    white and green
and wait for you to bloom and dry so I can
       taste you golden,
sweet and smooth, let you dance playfully
    in my cheeks
and warmly caress my velvet tongue. Slide
       down my throat,
and settle so I can breathe you all day,
    envelope me

in calm—a cup of you is just enough to
        let me know
that this crooked world is just as fine as
      your crooked smile
staring back at me from this chipped mug
        in a 5 a.m.
spoon-clanking diner in murky Manhattan.

IN GOD WE TRUST

The 7th Avenue Q station with its dank must
and hoards of bodies pushing turnstiles,
clanking and clomping stairs. all the while
the eye-patch guy shouts and jokes, hustling
change out of passersby. In God We Trust,
the all seeing eye pirate disguised, he smiles
as the crowd cranks their Ipod volume dials.
On the corner of Park and 7th Avenue they gust
by Ninja, a guy who sells junk and old bikes
in front of the liquor store at night. They pass
Rainer's frame shop where he worries and works
long hours, making rich people's art look nice,
a single dad of three cutting wood and glass
just trying to get by, for better or worse.

MUHAMMAD'S BODEGA

Muhammad is always working in the bodega on the corner
of Prospect and Underhill, yelling at his one small Hispanic
employee and people on the phone in Spanglish-Arabic.
Ringing up my cat litter and ice cream, he checks his anger
and tells me about his days getting up early to labor
on "Staten Island, then here," he says, cranky and manic
from living off four hours of sleep a night. Homesick,
he makes googly eyes when I stop by in my embroidered
Mexican dress. "They wear those in my country," he
says and tries to teach me "beautiful" in Arabic. I forget
it promptly, like any language I've ever tried to study.
"Teach me to read and write English." He eyes my body
as I grab my seltzer and scuttle out awkward, fretting
and longing for my good old New York anonymity.

CURMUDGEON SONG
For Winston

Gray hair clipped close to the skin, an air force pilot,
a German military sergeant, stern brow and fat cigar

surmising the scene. Post-traumatic sidewalk stress,
parallax sighting, I see metal grate shining with sun,

you-exploding shrapnel shudder. Throwing all twenty
pounds of your weight around, you quick sit down,

pavement paralyzed. Snarl and snap at puppies' sniff,
keeping us all in line, so no one plays or wanders

too far off the paths we've bludgeoned and beaten
in this tired earth. Classic cantankerous curmudgeon,

your wagging stump nub of a tail your only feeling
indication, usually still, seems to wag when you see

me coming and this is enough some days to keep
my troubled feet dry grass and weed answer combing.

THE BURROUGHS OF BROOKLYN

Summer in the Slope, the gray clouds hang low
over rooftop barbeque smoke. In Brooklyn, people
put plants on their roofs to pretend they have yards
where they watch the fireworks blast blue, red, white
on the 4th of July. The vines clogging my fire escape

my only green tonight. Saw the William Burroughs guy
the other day, the one who used to say, "Pardon me,
can you spare some change?" from a stoop on 7th
Avenue. I thought he'd died; maybe he just got clean,
though he still hobbles and nods, hunched over his cane.

Alyssa once tried to give him a fresh salad, he refused
muttering, "Capers? Disgusting, I have standards!"
We all have them, living in our tiny rotting apartments
in the big city so we'll always have something to do.
Restaurants with rats and caviar, movie theaters jammed

full of people watching Godard's Pierrot la Fou. Algerian
gangsters chasing Anna Karina and Jean-Paul Belmondo
painting his face blue, blowing himself up with primary-
colored dynamite. I trudge busy streets littered with trash,
and hate yet hope for rain to clear the clutter of all these
damn people and clean the piss and dirt off everything.

If someone says they've never thought about leaving
they're lying. The sky opens, drunk and spilling cold
all over everyone. Slowing down, people pause under
awnings praying it'll pass, this and all the other tough
things that worry them, so they can keep walking.

LAMPYRIDAE

Legs ache, face salt sweat, the kids are sprinkler
    screaming in the playground on Underhill,

a slow river of water leaks out onto the sidewalk,
    the dogs leave a path of wet paw prints

up the block. The June day wanes into cool night
    wisps of light in peripheral vision—I almost

forgot—once a year summer fireflies float me home
    and it almost makes this city living alright.

Lightning bug bioluminescent blasting away
    the buildings and bustle and I can pretend

it's just me in the woods away from jackhammers
    and jackasses, the nature ache hole in my chest

subsides for a second and I recall how at 22 all I wanted
    was concrete, but 10 years later all I want is green.

BANG LOUD LONG

We bang around Brooklyn summer streets' sticky
stink, trash cooking on the sidewalks in big black
bags. Past Fort Greene's flea market, stuffed racks
of old clothes and antiques. Further East we dally
past the rotting Navy Yard to Commodore Barry
Park to eat sweet plantains and shrimp and gawk
at African Art, listen to drumbeat thumps frantic.
Michael Jackson just died and his voice rings silky
from every barbeque boombox 2009, 4th of July.
Not even a day after his death, he's smiling up
from T-shirts on tables lining Court Street, right
next to Obama and urban novels in vast supply,
gotta make a living. Afro-punk skateboard worship
next to BAM, bands bang loud long into the night.

15-HOUR DRIVE TO NOTHING

Grey old Hutch winking through white curtains
    at me, foggy in his lime eye's cataract

cloud. He turns back to the window, watching
    tree leaves turn orange slow, from green

to gone within weeks. Winter is coming, not cold
    considering last summer. The band left me

dirty on a deserted Carolina street like some bad
    movie, beat from boxing and boulder-

bearing on broken shoulders alone, I lugged amps
    and played to exhaustion's breakdown

retreat. Head hung low, I heaved and staggered
    home. A 15-hour drive to nothing,

apartment trashed and robbed, guitar gone, character
    building. The police did nothing, hell-hot

sweating and swearing, seeking comfort I came
    to feed him for an absent friend and stayed

to sleep on the sofa in air conditioning. Curling
    consolation, he purred me to sleep.

The other cats, big Buster and bug-eyed Bug,
    formerly hiding, came out to investigate

me. So still, they sniffed gingerly, paws poked
    precise, to check I was still breathing.

MYSTERY WOMAN OF THE CONEY ISLAND CYCLONE

Metal clanking chinkity *chink chink chink*
and wood saw splinter? Gravity pulls
shoulders back, eyes to the sky's lemon-
apple sun, sweet-sour. To the top, hear
the children scream arms raised up, I cling,
been riding this coaster too long, the thrill's
gone all out of its dips and spins. Seen
the vomit spills of Nathan's Hotdogs
since 1959 and the fires licking Steeplechase
beams to singe. Seen the Freak Show's
men with their tattoos walking the grounds,
just making the rounds. This coaster's dives
and white-red paint peel makes me lonesome
for my old dives and my skin before windburn
and sun stripped my bones clean. If only I had
windows to close with shades to draw
and a bathtub for gin. A heart shaped house
that doesn't shake as easily as the framework
of me. How 'bout a yard to toe-tickle barefoot,
grass to hay—good for a roll in with a man?
Maybe I can remember I have a body before
it's too late? But I fear that my plates will always
have to spin on these old sticks—another smash
and the pieces probably won't glue back quite right.
Maybe another passenger would blow the sticky
sting instead of just blowing the scene? Maybe
he'd be tall and sweet, stop this ride so we could
watch the firecrackers bang to thin pieces of colored
tissue rain from the cloudy puff of smoke on a July's eve.

TEETH AND TAXES

Sini buzzes up on Queenie, her little white Aprilla
scooter two stoops down. The stray cats car dive
under, hide until the white-blonde tattooed Buddha
quiets her motor, extinguishing bright light drive.
The cats sneak back by, Stripes and Gray, the tribe.
Sini scratches snipped ears as they food beg, street
cat in her own right. Teeth torture, she's survived,
torn from the gums one by one after years of concrete
neglect, childhood Chicago project rat kissing sleep
and alcoholism. She smokes under orange streetlights,
we talk about God and Coney Island Fridays beneath
the fireworks and screaming cyclone freaks, nights
of Nathan's tiny red fork crinkled accordions salt
consuming ocean swims, the small thrills we now exalt.

SIDEWAYS BRAIN REFRAIN
For Alyssa

"That girl thinks she's the queen of the neighborhood.
I got news for you, she is!" First words spoken, eight
years later still friends, though so much has changed.
You've transitioned male to female, misunderstood
by many, in Sunset Park gay bashed on the train.
Saving umbrella skeletons from the street after rain,
room of wax and paint gone after your family stood
in court and lost the house on 2nd Street. Childhood
gone, we ponder the monsters that shook our brain
chemicals so sideways. We listen to old punk records,
and see movies at BAM on Saturdays, talk writing-
my silly dog poems and your crazy Beckett plays.
Your old Pogo jokes and tongue sharp as swords,
my wry saunter suspicious of everything, trudging
around Brooklyn's gummy summer street malaise.

MY ARTILLERY HEART

For Inga

You must not fight too often with one enemy, or you will
teach him all your art of war." —NAPOLEON BONAPARTE

Dark horse racing, my trusted confidant, my second in command,
    most admired admiral, give me the Blitzkrieg, the strategy

of exhaustion. Would that she could read Proust wearing spectacles,
    running fingers through hair over a cappuccino in some French

café. Then wisecrack dance on bars joy drunk falling night, lit diamond
    white, gleaming from her bejeweled chest of light and arrowheads

sharp. Mischief maker maneuvers, hungry meat hunt and chase each other,
    we hallway hide, seek, slip, slide. But this life is no game of Risk

with its colorful cardboard and plastic pieces. That man has my artillery
    heart on the Maginot line. His mounted archers drawing, Sun Tzu

Schwerpunkt shooting squad. Finger itchy ironclad infantry stick trigger
    of his casemates concrete interior invasion, barbed wire fortification.

I touch tactical, launch the trench trebuchet, scare him, smoke him out
    of his hole, my grand strategy-surprise diplomacy, restore

democracy to his tyranny. I beg of you to bark down his blockade,
    you control the corps and cavalry, cut them off at the knees.

His jaw makes me too whisker weak to charge at the front with my steam-
    powered platoon, foam frustrated mouth of machine guns

and machetes sharp tongue cuts. Defensive divisions, can we get past
    our offensive opinions? Sprint the checked board to stalemate.

EAST RIVER WALK-TALK

We take these epic walks from Fifth Avenue
in the Slope, to street fairs in Carroll Gardens.
selling the same socks and jewelry, African
masks and homemade lemonade along Smith
Street. We keep going through Cobble Hill
to Brooklyn Heights, sit on the promenade
and look at Manhattan's lower toothy grin
where no one goes but tourists, businessmen,
and commuters from Staten Island. We watch
the ships chug slowly by under clouds and blue
then keep walking to Dumbo to the ice cream
shop with the long lines, walk amongst the old
brick warehouse buildings where Whitman
once wrote for the Daily Eagle, make our way
to Brooklyn Bridge Park to sit in the grass
and watch the same old guy in the banana
yellow thong sunning himself to onlookers'
giggles. Then head up onto the bridge trying
not to look down through the wooden slats
at the river deep below, to South Street Seaport
where we sit in wooden lounge chairs thinking
about how long it took us to finally get here,
stare at where we came from, and you say,
"All I want is to sit by the water with you."

JONAH

Like sleeping under a lawnmower, you buzz and clank
busted heating pipes between our heads, grooming
our hair, a silly stylist with your slimy sandpaper tongue.
We wake to examine our strange coifs in the bathroom
mirror, leave the water running for you to drink, baptizing
your grey striped head. Found splashing in a puddle,
they named you Jonah and you took refuge in Dennis,
your soft mew becoming his conscience, following
him room to room like some little specter insisting
on being part of the action. Up in Washington Heights,
you smart strut toilet trained yourself, but downtown
in Brooklyn began going in your water dish misguidedly
thinking you're doing the right thing. We fill tall glasses
of water for you to drink, as they empty you start running
in place scratching up the wood floor. You dig your way
to China in your litter box, cram yourself into paper bags
and boxes too small for your meaty frame, lie by the open
refrigerator panting summers away. Run up to the roof
to chase pigeons and stare at the skyline—the clock tower
and lady liberty slowly getting covered up by the ugly new
buildings growing higher and higher along fourth avenue.
Now like our green girl in the harbor you're suddenly gone
and our insides are empty like God's great blue whale.

DIESEL GHOSTS

Horizon cranes tower over quiet water, industrial
giraffes in a bucolic oasis. Red Hook's halcyon
from the cacophonous city's screech, an asylum.
Seagulls sing a sea shanty echo above the diesel
ghosts of sailors smoking on rusted wench axle.
Barking dogs chase thrown sticks into water, agile
on the jagged beaches. Ducks swim their kingdom,
tails twitching on by old trolley lines, the chasm
of time. Beard's Brick Warehouse lines the channel
guarding the shore from more condos. The Merchant
Stores full of plants' green and key lime pie's sweet-
sour tongue sting, milk paint above reads the same
as 1920—Lemon-lime, Root Beer, and Cream. Distant
Lady Liberty stern stares back at us as tugboats fleets
float past, she holds her torch ready to set us aflame.

POUGHKEEPSIE POEM

Toad Hall with its twists and turns, bathrooms opening
into other bathrooms, old servants' quarters low ceilings,
stairs slope and wind back into the kitchen. Turkeys
and frogs croak in the yard of green, lightning bugs
and dancing mosquitoes buzz. We hike through ticks
and flowered fields of Poet's Walk, sit in old wooden
gazebos and stare at the Hudson River, shop at grocery
stores that classify Green Tea as "New Age Beverages,"
drive dizzy roads to Opus 40 stones in the Saugerties,
a monument tomb to obsessive sculpture. It's raining,
steam rises off the hot rocks as if ready for dark-cloaked
druid sacrificing. Locust Grove's rolling lawns and gardens,
house of servant's ghosts and carriages, the Young's pet
cemeteries headstones marked Snappy and Rusty. Back
in the city in coffee shops surrounded by people on cell
(as in jail) phones talking. I'm longing for quiet lakes
and green away from laptops and technology's electric bars.

PASSIVE RESISTANCE
for Phoebe C.

You thought you'd found a home, wandering
through the park woods alone, stumbled upon
your green-eyed sucker and let out a loud
smoker's mew. "Who's gonna take her?"
All eyes on Dennis, late to school as a kid
cause of stopping to say hi to all the animals
along the way, he grumbled as scooped you up
carried you home. Back to the apartment
with that big oaf Jonah, you got him in line
until—at last—his time was up. Finally,
you and Dennis were alone for about a week
and then I came busting in with Itty Pity in tow.
She started out scared up on top of the kitchen
cabinets and then came down from her mountain
to chase you away anytime you get too close
to *her* humans. You sit silent in the bathroom
on the side of the tub and stare sadly at the wall,
waiting for someone to come turn the faucet on.
And then the fucking growling dog, with the *same*
name as you moves in, and we have to keep
the windows closed to keep you from throwing
yourself out. You settle for passive aggressive
revenge—knocking over the dirty litter box
when we're not home. Puking on us in bed
in the middle of the night, Dennis tries valiantly
to wake up and catch it in his hand to save the sheets
but, inevitably, it slips through his fingers
and we're both up grumbling. All he wants
for the years of kibble fed and ears scratched
is for all of us to sit on the couch together
in a giant furry pile in this crazy place we call home.

ELEPHANT ON BROOKLYN BRIDGE

We argue over bridges and subway routes.
You think riding the Q train over the Manhattan
Bridge is best 'cause you can see the Staten
Island ferry and city lights spilling through
the window scratchiti, lines swimming newts
and abstract minnows in a tank, children's
drawings. I say walking over the Brooklyn
Bridge is best, its limestone arches portals to
the past and future. Forgotten, the Roeblings
and PT Barnum sent Jumbo trotting over
to prove it was safe. Today, you and I
in suspension between two lives hanging
on, don't look down at feet or the river under.
Look up, there are elephants floating in the sky.

THESE STREETS AREN'T ZAGAT RATED

The Lower East Side once tenements and turbulence,
the Ramones at CBGBs and all the other flophouse
drunks and bums on the Bowery, now glasshouse,
high-priced condos and galleries and the cadence
of jackhammers and wrecking balls. Old residents
protests no matter, those big money folks trounce
everyone and everything. Neighborhoods once
thrived, no more, chain stores mark the absence
of once great family businesses. New York is
becoming like the suburban sprawl we all fled
here to escape. The art and music moved East
to Williamsburg. Broadway is dimming its lights,
shutting down, recession bound. We've bled
dry, pulled teeth, devoured this city like beasts.

LAUNDROMAT LADIES

Pushing wire black granny carts full of clothes
   down the street amidst old gray snow
   turned to ice, slippery, 19 degrees, still

they come. These ladies of the old Vanderbilt
   laundromat got a system, man. Special
   soaps and softeners spin in silver

machines. Not just a chore, an event, taking
   up six machines, trash talking
   and guarding space, real estate

in this city such a commodity. These ladies
   believe in separating whites, darks,
   bath towels, sheets, dropping wet socks

on the scratched up floor. Like some desert
   Reno Casino, change clanks and clinks
   through the metal slots of the Laundry Bar

soap machine from the seventies, its orange
   and brown letters fading and ironically
   unclean. The dryers sparse and framed

by fake plastic wood paneling spark bickering
   over bathmats at the folding station.
   A handwritten sign on the wall reads,

We're not responsible for any damages,
   I wonder if the laundromat turf war
   ever drove these ladies to blows.

Please, no dirty clothes in the baskets.
   What about dogs? Out of time,
   I pick up Stella and wheel her

around, She doesn't mind, she's happy
to go anywhere, anytime. Shaking
from Gorilla Coffee's caffeine spin,

I burn fingers shoving steaming clothes
fresh from the dryer into my
old green army rucksack.

The Chinese ladies who run the joint
can't decide whether to yell
at me for the dog or laugh.

Instead they giggle at some guy shivering
in his shorts, unloading his clothes.
He mutters, "Everything's dirty."

GENESIS
for Phoebe D aka Gooby

Our love began with you growling at me wedged
behind a toilet—I had to use the plunger to force
you out—so many teeth for such a little thing.
Or maybe it was at that sunny waterfront park
in Poughkeepsie where you rolled in goose shit
and came grinning back to me proudly. I washed
you off in the bathroom sink in the train station
while the ladies in line laughed. Dennis rolled
his eyes when he saw you—a wet, skinny rat.
Or was it when you ran up a Catskill mountain
taunting us and taking your sweet ass time
to prance back down covered in spiky fur burrs
I had to pick out one by one. Back at the house
in Saugerties you tried to chase the horses
next door convinced they were an enemy
needing to be thwarted. Then there was the time
we were driving and you tried to snuggle me,
as I pushed you away I almost hit the guardrail,
So many near missed accidents since you picked
me out with your boney, blonde little paw.

SLOPE

"I'm not much for gossiping, but I do like to talk shit."
The Slope Opera's in full swing, so-and-so is coming
out in full lesbian fashion. So-and-so's shift missing
got them expelled from the Food Co-op. No more

fresh greens, crowded shelves, long communist lines.
Walking along 7th Avenue, Bones, a bearded tough
motorcycle guy, drives by in his little pink Barbie
car while stroller moms saunter and stare hogging up

the sidewalk. Dogs stop and sniff Marty's restaurant,
La Taqueria, with its psychedelic murals and burly
bean burritos, but pass on by pulling to Prospect Park
to bound around off leash and swim at dog beach

(which is really just the edge of a lake). I walk on
to browse the crowded shelves of the Community
Bookstore. I step over the two old dogs sleeping
by the new release hardcovers and head to the poetry

section. Run my fingers along the colorful spines,
huff the dust and ink and all the musty spent sweat
of the writers who've gone before me. I search to see
who I'll be sandwiched between when it's my time

up on that wall with all the language queens and kings.
Beside me to one side perhaps orphan Corso bopping
with the Beats, *The Bridge* of Hart Crane, and old ee
in all his eccentric glory. To the right this tenderness

comes from Mark Doty, Rita Dove's smart line struts
on by Denise Duhamel's sassy sestinas. All of us up
there together getting dusty on the shelf pressed tight
together our slick, sharp corners softening with time.

THE CIRCUS IS IN TOWN

Brooklyn is sirens squealing, drills pounding
concrete and beeping trucks' brakes screech.
Even the littlest birds scream in Brooklyn,
the sparrows with their tiny brown bodies
and mighty lungs. No chirping beautiful songs,
just pigeons cooing and pooing. Hammers
pounding, subways clanking underground,
and people talking, oh my god, the things
they say: "No wonder he gave you a cigarette,
girl, with yo' big sweaty-ass fun bags hanging out."
"He's a bad kisser, and he has a brain tumor"
"I get shunned by this world run by douche bags."
(That last one was me) I duck into Gorilla Coffee
with its music blasting, espresso machines clicking,
and milk steam shriek. I've shivered whole winters
away at these red tables writing, trying to right
wrongs wired in my head. The noise outside
is nothing compared to the blasting inside my brain,
in this life the only enemy I have is my own mind.
Head to the Q train, somewhere between Atlantic
and Dekalb a kid starts to scream "Papi, I've never
been to the circus! I want to go to the circus!"
In New York kid, trust me, you're already here.

2.
DOGS OF
BROOKLYN

THE DOGS OF BROOKLYN

I never dreamed I'd scrape my living walking dogs,
chasing tails in circles amidst rusted water towers
and brownstones. Pavement pound, gray stray cat
pounce, takes a swing at surprised pups who bark
and bound at his tough guy swagger. A Brooklyn
chat noir shadow, he sits just out of reach, jumps

and mocks lack of leash length. Pepper, jumping
black Shepard, shrieks and shrinks, city dogs
school quickly, their minds no match for Brooklyn
bullying sharp feline streets. The buildings tower
over this scene, big brown Gods observing barks
like deaf guards. Bored, our *gato* slinks off, a delicate

sniff, to sift through the trash, meets another cat
striped and skinny to search and share a meal. Jumps
belly full to mark his territory, rubs his scent on the bark
of an old tree, its roots cracking cement. The dogs,
foiled again walk on, heads down defeated. I tower
over this sad show and think of days before Brooklyn

when all seemed out of reach, but then—ah Brooklyn—
all the possibility! Its bustling blocks, an intricate
painting of neighbors chatting on stoops, kids in tow
sidewalk chalk hopscotch drawing and clumsy jumping
from box 1 to 2 to 3. Fugetaboutit, excited the dogs
hop too, do a maypole dance around me as I bark

at them to calm down. Prospect Park bound, barking
hounds pick up pace pulling and wagging. Brooklyn
beasts off leash dance free as I write this doggerel.
They mud puddle splash on the long meadow, cats
now out of mind, hunt squirrels never catching, jumping
perros chase and show off their speed as birds tower

tweet their alarm *retreat, retreat, retreat!* Their towers
invaded by these acorn stealing hairy sneaks, up bark
scuttling. *Did someone say treat?* The dogs jumping
barrel over to me expectantly, ears up at Brooklyn's
loud siren songs summoning. We head home, cat
sniffing and panting tiredly. Oh, to be like the dogs

happy just for the hunt. They don't need towers
and lists of cats they've conquered. They're jumping
just to bounce around Brooklyn barking loud and free.

BULLS OF PAMPLONA
For Thurgood

Lost in this world, led only by leash. Your last peek
    the gray triangle of mountain peak, salt-ocean

waves brutal beat, summer seared-sun outline of busy
    Brooklyn streets. Blinked black and it was all

gone. No one explained the darkness. You just accepted
    it and moved on, slithering along rough brick

building lines, their smooth cool insides. Stumbling
    step and stump, wall bang-bump clumsy,

til' the hair scraped from your skull, holes in your gray
    grinning strands and spikes, easier ear scratch.

Before you, I was two years blind. Lost sense, music
    ears pricked, but fingertips felt for blades in back—

no sensation. Flames licked feet asleep beneath a shivering
    half-deck house of cards burning. Sniffed the char,

licked ashes but tasted nothing. Only the beautiful screech
    of guitar feedback and tinnitus ring and thump

of locust drums beat until your excited shrill scold and bark
    for being left alone sniffing around for that damn

cat who's always just one step and eight lives ahead woke me.
    Reckless abandon until then, launched the Chupinaxo,

we ran full boar, bulls of Pamplona bucking bodies buckle
    into the encierro. Broken broncos beat a *Fuck it*

into fences. The crash came too soon. We sat, legs splayed,
    stunned. For the first time, I felt your soft ears

and rubbed the collision from your head as you nuzzled
    your impact into my palm. Lying there, we smelled

the cut grass and the sun. We crawled from the crevice
    where we'd crammed ourselves to sleep safely.

Forced to feet, we learned to walk slow feeling our feet
    notice steps and green growing though cracked

and soiled cement. As we paced the parkway sirens sang
    and signaled us to hear outside our heads'

cacophony. Short sight lengthening, we taste spring
    and all the growth that the cold rain brings.

CASTLE QUEEN

Olive sleeps squished up in a fruit bowl on the kitchen
counter, her striped and spotted tail swishing over its
ceramic side, taunting. After hours, she wakes to case

the *clank* of the front fence gate. No hurry, she stretches
long and yawns, slowly making her way. Ginger's ears
perk at the stir and *thunk* of kitten kitchen table pranks.

Ten years castle queen then along this coy cat came,
sauntering around like she owns the place. Ginger's
toenails click on the wooden floor as she investigates.

From nowhere a white paw socks her muzzle gray.
She jumps back barking and looks up to find Olive's
tiny frame towering over *her* dog, mocking. Quick,

to the window chase! Distracted, retaliation will have
to wait while they contemplate all of the people out on
the sidewalk marching in time trying to keep pace.

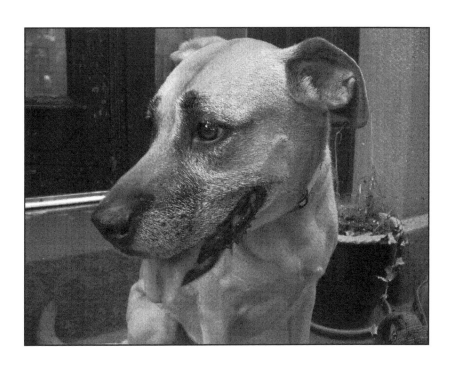

THE MYTHICAL BEAST OF BROOKLYN
For Mico

I got a picture of you in the mail before I even met you. I showed
it to Tim and he said, "I don't get it," meaning you. Cacophonous
cuts of creatures collaged into one. Your tail an exotic fan, a peacock
      plume, black and fine. A white cross carved into your chest

like a medieval knight sent by God to save us from the savages.
Black triangle back, Ace of Diamonds, you're one card short,
with your orange crown of fur and ears you were meant to play
      the clown. A mad jester to make us laugh since Dela left

town. She's off nuzzling all the ones that left us, and bark-bossing
all the playing angel pups to slow down. Spider monkey eyes
and claws, Muppet puppet polka dot paws do your little tap dance
      on me while I sleep. You taunt your sister Tana towering

majestically atop me. You are king of the Dogsitter mountain
that is me groaning, pulling sheets over my head as your paws
squish kidneys to spine. But what is this distraction? Tana, that sly
      little fox, steals your bone and you're down again dethroned,

chasing your minion all around until your royal scepter is found.
Overnight, you leave me "presents"; one sleepy misstep my feet
turn brown. Wake to clean, the big city no place for a wilderness
      pup, you've chewed the floorboards to splinter. We take

to the streets, you're pulling to choke leash, with your goofy grin
of triangle white teeth you eagerly greet the Manhattan bound stiff
suits, As they strut the sidewalk, their robot clank of footsteps breaks
      as they shimmy away from the mythical beast of Brooklyn.

EASY'S HARD

Easy isn't easy, he's hard, throws his weight around
like a sack of wet laundry, stopping to sniff anything

that strikes his fancy. Fat feet strut, tripping over
his dopey ears dragging on the ground. A good guy

just growing into his oversized head and body,
undersized legs busy trying to keep up, wanting

to be bigger so badly. Basset Hound sound a whine
anytime he finds another of his kind to hop around

with. I have to coax, cajole, con him on. He lays down,
sluggish, like these lines I write. Slows me down, eating

snow and smelling everything, and maybe that's what
I need. In too much of a hurry most of the time, the fear

I'm missing something makes me miss what's in front
of me. Frustration falls, I let him lead and see the snow

glow on the buildings, the quiet of the usually loud streets,
enjoy the journey, we'll get where we're going eventually.

(MON)TANA A.K.A. HOLLYWOOD

Berry blonde lashes split waterfalls
over liquid brown eyes. Underbite
smile a snarl to the untrained eye.

Bored beauty, you yawn a tongue
of pink wet ribbon curl extending.
We go for a walk, you hula-hoop

a flirty schoolgirl white sock hop.
The neighborhood kids' grubby
fingers find you. A miniature army

assault, you scramble eggs away,
your teeth, sharp shell shards showing.
A misstep, I crush a porcelain paw.

A shriek, a scream, you've been hit,
you fall to the pavement—a gunshot
victim. People stare from their stoops

sourcing the sounds of sin. You writhe,
I apologize, stroke your striped nose
and tail, a goofy snow-tipped crescent

moon. Alert the Academy, Hollywood
actors can't hold a candle. Lon Chaney's
Hunchback limp lacked your conviction,

though your fiction keeps switching sides.
You cast mournful glances out the corners
of your eyes as we make the long trot home.

ST. FRANCIS OF 42ᴺᴰ STREET

Troubador turned beggar, a dapper king growling from your jeweled
throne as I enter your home. You turn your whiskered nose up
     until I offer mice bites of cheese from the icebox.

You take them carefully from my fingertips with your tiny teeth,
then to show your love of all creatures great and small, you hump
     your giraffe. Our pilgrimage begins, we step out amidst

the Poor Clares, you sniff gingerly. Slip and click, claws scrape
hallway linoleum as you scuttle from doormat to doormat. Sit
     your silent protest of passive resistance at top of stairs—

it worked for Ghandi and Martin Luther King but you're just ten
tough pounds of hair and teeth, a bat without wings, this city's
     great rat terrier, terrorist king. Jacob's not the only one

who's wrestling bigger things. I coax you downward, you resist
then relent, sensing my stubbornness more than your own.
     On the streets you're a bowling ball on a string, a yo-yo

getting caught on the scents of trees and your need to mark
everything, a urinary graffiti artist bombing the hell out
     of Brooklyn, needing to be smelled and seen,

and then comes a Shepard, a flock of other dogs, and you snap
from your cool collar upturned James Dean to the 42ⁿᵈ street
     savage yelling and foaming. You may need to rethink

your recruitment strategy. I lift you up in your harness—suspended
you squirm a spider web worn and traveling. A flight of steps,
     a plight of depths, stop dead in your tracks afraid of falling

upwards. It's let go or be dragged, you're rising, surprising yourself
with your own abilities, if only walking through fear was as easy
     as being pulled up by someone who keeps believing.

CREW OF BUCCANEERS

Pirate dogs on parade, my faithful first mate longs
for a peg leg. Toby teeters on his three paws pausing

along Eastern Parkway. Its loud traffic whooshing by;
shut your eyes hard enough and you'll hear waves.

Jumping on his head like some hooligan cabin boy
gone wrong, Jasper the one-eyed whippit-beagle pup

prance-plunders our patience, leash linked, no escape.
Monkey-pawed marauder sly with his patchless permanent

wink, roves and raids this sea beach of cement and green
for treasure, Jolly Roger chicken bones to chomp-chew.

I'm Anne Bonny groaning *ARR!* at my crew of buccaneers,
a poet privateer pillaging lines for sea songs, a raconteur

swashbuckling adventure out of the everyday. None of us
knows what marvels await, bewilderment just a block away.

EINSTEIN AND DON KING

For Roxy and Finster

Waiting for the keys to drop, a crazy mix of pig and caterpillar
 bug big-eyed pug jump-lick snorting at my shins ignore,

heart-worming his way beneath my skin. His territorial Terrier
 sidekick slithers out from under bed combat style

sleeping off morning reconnaissance missions, stumbles
 into the hall hangover weary. Gray hair matted

yet stuck up, a mix of Einstein and Don King dreaming up
 equations and ready for the fight to begin. Barking

off other dogs on the sidewalk sending them into foaming panic.
 Winter snow dramatic, dogsled scaling dirty slush tundra,

summer spent snorting pant as if crossing the Sahara screaming,
 "Water!" and "We're not gonna make it!" Legs splayed

out behind flat belly cooling on shady concrete. Downstairs paw
 chomp and play, pause-stare and crash again. Who knew goofs

could be my best teachers? On my command, able to sit indifferent
 while anti-social pups agonize out of reach longing to lunge

at you. I calm and quiet their fit, let them solicitously sniff you, still
 and steady until they're wagging at finally finding friends.

AWKWARD TEENAGE STRIDE

For Charlie

Patience perched beneath dark curlicue vines
of eighties metal hair. Black marble eyes
peep aside a schnoz his face never grew into.

Chained neck, I picture him in torn Metallica
T-shirts, over-grooming sharp fingernails
like the guitar guys at my high school used to.

Awkward teenage stride, paranoid pacing war
veteran always looking behind, lazy-stoned
smile. Tail, a fountain of hair shooting up

out of ass and falling down again, a cheerleader's
limp pompom, a furry Dr. Seuss palm tree
swaying in the salt ocean breeze. A hurricane—

your sidekick Chloe, a swollen fox, a mouse
with a giant orange afro and a Gene Simmons
tongue, reptile-long licking air tasting ice. Bill

and Ted's Excellent Adventure of the animal
kind, twenty-degree frozen winter no matter,
they wait for walks staring as if I've told a joke

and forgotten the punch line. My akimbo arms
pulled into night, Chloe climbs Charlie's legs
long vines, an ebullient bully, threatening as a dust

bunny. He missteps, feign fright faking—the mark
of a big one is that they let the little ones think
they're winning the war some of the time.

WRESTLING A CERBERUS
For Shorty, Lucky, and T-bone

For years depression's imaginary demons have doused darkness
over my eyes. Through pinpricks I peeked at their many haired

heads taunting from the foot of the bed. Biting toes and brewing
coffee before I wake, ready to tear me through the day. Unphased

by daemon ways, when their flesh and blood cousins appeared,
I was only slightly surprised by these se'irim. Shorty, Rakshasa

disguised as Yorkie, brave and true snuck up to sniff my shoe.
Not much bigger than my foot he scuttled a black brown blur

as I started to move. Tiharire T-bone, the glamorous blonde
daeva hanging out on the bed waiting to be impressed or carried

around, stared, but couldn't be bothered to receive me. Asura
Lucky, loudly guarded the other two, barking and balking,

a dancing daschund, all talk. I lean to leash and he sinks
to the ground peeing, piddling around. I leash the other two

and find I have a three-headed hydra on my hands. Cerberus
hellhounds, have their tricephalic argument zigzagging around

getting nowhere. I have to lead them in their hop run down
the sidewalk. Shorty and Lucky competing for the lead, T-bone

dragging behind. Lucky's tail, a feather plume, a flag—jolly roger
warning of this ship of fools. I'm in stitches, laughing, grabbing

guts at my ridiculous predicament. Even jinn have been known
to save a few. Hercules wrestled, Orpheus serenaded, Hermes,

Sybil, and Psyche soothed to sleep, add me to the mythology.
Hades hounds let me out of hell for giving them a bathroom break.

COMET IN LOVE

"He's a humper!" Melissa's message read.
    I was off gallivanting, getting crabs

not from humping but from sleeping
    in dirty dorm beds in Prague,

when Comet descended upon us. He hit
    Brooklyn like a bomb, a pint-sized

wiener dog missile skidding to a stop
    in his squat-legged , black brindle

spotted funny hop run. Fresh from upstate
    streets and shelter, helter skelter,

a four-time runaway taken in by a family
    with a precocious kid living

in a converted school building, P.S. 9,
    on Vanderbilt and Sterling,

learning new lessons under its lush vines
    overgrown and clinging like him

to anything strong and standing still
    in this world's constant spinning.

We teach him, tame him until, surprise,
    Pepper's not spayed, she's in heat!

A big black beauty, German Shepard
    shrieking and shying away

from Comet crazed and careening
    his angry red crayon

on his tippy-toes in a pheromone haze
    trying to force fatherhood.

Could he reach, what strange babies
    they'd make. Neutered, no matter

to his raging biology. He's twelve pounds
    of terror trailing his large German

mistress down the street. I can relate,
    in a world out of control alone

clinging and clamoring for any home
    or family one can make despite

whatever crushing or pummeling your
    tiny frame may have to take.

SPACE INVADERS

White Westie waiting not wanting to walk, Bella bellows
low to the ground at the sound of my keys in the door.

Upon my entrance she lies still like a squirrel just spotted
in her, "If I don't move they can't see me" hide and seek.

Upstairs to the jailed puppy-beast, Sheperd-beagle mix
of unknown origins, alien Zigzag unleashed gallops

a galumph down stairs flight to a fight. Bella, a growling
girl wondering when they're taking this dumb dog back

to wherever the hell he came from. Outside, Ziggy observes
everything through the mouth—sticks, rocks, glass, leash

I pry open his jaw and remove the menagerie, his brown
eyes screwed up in his skull gazing up at me. He retreats,

jumping on and licking the brown Brownstone renovating
construction guys as they try to eat their fast-food lunches

on the stoop; they giggle like little kids loving this softness
in their hard hands. Bella drags behind stopping stubborn

sniffing marking her way to get back home in case of escape
from the retarded rabbit pup and the strict dog-bossing matron.

PSYCHIC ELECTRICIANS
For Lucy

She paces floors protecting doors and sleeping child sweet
inside. Tail and ears low, flat-back growl, bone's calcium
chew rattles teeth within hollow echo of mouth's pink.

Shy liquid eyes pendulum swing, mind read. My feet sink
into street concrete, shoulders tight-high, tense, tattered cap
covering covert eyes, keeping out the sun and other bright

things. Cocked gun, cracked knuckle, crime victim heart
in witness protection. Clock clicks a metronome beat,
chased chaste hide, you seek. Sensing the safety of me,

she collapses on the hallway floor- writhing body a flop
fish flip, blinking gills gasping air; wagging tail a ship
rudder steering boats mad, circling waters' dark and deep

below, catfish and torpedo rays swimming there. We coy
strut streets ahoy! Sniffing ants antsy, she sucks sticks
from the sidewalk chomping to calm. I scribble shuffle

paper stacks, getting it out while keeping it all in. We read
energy like religious texts, psychic electricians rewiring
fictions we no longer believe. Rubbing rods of amber static

we attract amorous accomplices, we wrestle chests wide wading
slow tiptoe into a warm pool of dopamine flow. We glow
incandescent no longer fighting magnetic fields' push and pull.

DOGBORGS BOLT JOLT

Hoser and Chloe howl and honk strange dinosaur
noises nurtured by necklace chains of electroshock
therapy fuse boxes, electric vampire bark-ZAP-
charge and whine. Cyborg technology, they've
adapted their language like some tribe stranded
in a foreign country, communicating voltaic
translation. Their house a minefield—lightning
bolt volt bounce couch jolt, shock pad torches
toes kite flying Benjamin Franklin strike electricity,
AC/DC on off on. Hard-wiring, circuits unbroken
robotica, they charge the magnetic treat bowl
after wild walks of leash pulling to mark everything.
Yellow and black blurs sit still, brows raised, ears
perked like exclamation marks, technically behaving.

FROG DOG HOP

Bailey tripod hops down his steps past the primary
color neon of the comic book shop. He's a cartoon
dog be-bopping along 7th Avenue batting eyelashes

at anyone who might happen to look his way or not.
This frog dog hurdles for the Haagen Daz Ice cream
shop on the corner of President Street, crumb lunges

and pleads pets from the people sitting on the benches
outside laughing and licking their melting cones of butter
pecan and rocky road, we're all trudging. We sleuth-

search the streets' many mysteries, Brooklyn's blocks
bloom flowering trees, intricacies, and history ever-
changing. Bailey breaks, flopping down on the hot

concrete until another dog passes by then he trick
heaves tripping alarm from this terrier. Friend found,
they dodge and bounce around, their only time is now.

POPSICLE AUGUST

For Pepper

The only German dog I've met who isn't bossy. Menacing
    shine-white teeth cave stalagmites and stalactites.

Orange brown eyes much like mine, small sprightly spirit
    in big body all limbs and elbows. Part German

shepherd, part Saharan wolf, Egyptian goddess jackal Anput,
    Anubis, God of the dead til' Osiris knocked you off

your throne. Walking with Isis, shepherding her along, dancing
    in circles leading the blind. Weighing hearts on your scales

of justice, feeding the wicked to Ammit sipping souls straining
    and sucking through straws. Weigh my heart heavy

with time and lines strung to the earth rip chord, full of hot air
    and hard stares into darkness. Orchestrating mummies,

choreographer of the dancing dead. Conductor of souls, lead
    me back from these hot days of popsicle August.

We pant and walk close to the ground sneaking around the sun.

RACE RELATIONS

Pippa whispers to me, "Chile and Luna are racist."
Their burly blonde bodies have been getting fat
fetching bacon from their beneficent black neighbor
who sizzles salty strips of lard for these Labradors.
Now they drool and wag wildly, amble up to any
ample ebony man on the street expecting greasy
treats but are greeted by shrieks and cursing
"Man, get those dogs the hell away from me!"

Sally shuns and scorns basket ball bouncing
brown kids on her block whooping. Pincher
Miniature, Napoleonic noise-miser, a little
thing, she's learned the art of pounce projecting,
her boisterous bark booming off the buildings
on Lincoln Place sending children caterwauling
and hopping from her hateful hullabaloo, while

Fred and Harry hate their neighbor Pepper,
the black German Shepard (Is there even
such a thing as a black German?). Perhaps
descended from dogs of the European Union,
griping grandparents who relegated WWII
tales between tail chewing. Harry teeth bares,
and Fred, these days after cancer, looking
like a war veteran hobbles up on his three legs
just to bawl at her as her big body bails fighting
out the front door frustrated from guarding
Schmack the gray cat indoors all day, she longs
for more mission action, machine guns firing.

Pepper once barked at a Hasidic man, a building
Super putting out the trash on Tuesday. She got
one look at the white tassel tzitzis taunting,
hanging from his pants and despite the beauty
of their meaning—God being everywhere
in the four directions East, South, West, North—
she disagreed. Perhaps an atheist, or the fashion
police, she lunged, I snapped her rubber band
spring dance back apologizing. "Sorry,
she's German." I joked, and he laughed too.

MEXICAN DOGS

For Canela and Lucky

We are free here to dig through the trash;
to break through plastic bag skin to savor
    strained beans and tough tortilla,

to bark and scratch our matted mange,
to pounce at strange Great-tailed Grackles
    and gatos who get in our way.

The people here ignore us like pigeons
picking at crumbs in the city square,
    they don't even see us anymore.

We nurse our pups in abandoned houses,
we sleep in when it rains. At the beach
    in Celestun we search for crabs

in the sand and score crackers from Gringos
who think we're sick and sad, they're suckers.
    We'd rather hunt wild prey or starve

than eat kibble every day, run than be leashed
and forced to sit on command. We'll take our
    chances, going anywhere we can.

BRAVE MONKEY DANCE

Plucked from the Puerto Rican archipelago,
the oldest and smallest Tibetan holy dog,
Shih Tzu, Sammy. A baby snow lion,

a chrysanthemum we took to calling crusty
'cause of your snub-nosed eating, dried meat
clinging to furry cheeks. Court jester snorting

pranks, running hallways home, deranged rabbit
dashing, short legs shooting out behind. Old
curmudgeon man, ass planted defiant under bite

grin, refusing to walk and the silly hop back
into pack stride as you realize I'm bigger,
stronger, and a lot more stubborn than you.

Brave monkey dance enticing play from the big
dogs, bouncing and barking like a village savage.
A stealth sleeper, hiding in suitcases, closets, under

loft beds, staring down from spiral staircases. Teddy
bear terror snuggling as though burrowing into skin
parasitic, a love sucking tick nestling in the armpit.

POWERBOAT PIT BULL
For Eva

Cartoon paws spread web-wide, wiggle
a little two-step upon arrival. A brindle-
brown wild tigress, snakeskin sheen,
slithering along the walls of Brooklyn

> buildings. Nosing my knees, knocking
> legs out beneath or hammerhead sharking
> shins shiny amethyst wine. Street thugs
> saunter and say, "Hey, nice Pit." Tail

between legs, Cowardly Lion, eyes wide,
ears perked, city construction sounds
and strangers scary. You powerboat-pull
me, pavement water-skier, into Lucy's lair.

> She's your best girl, block buddy, partner
in grime. You rocket launch upstairs amidst
> laughing doorman Rudolpho's stares, drag
me tripping upwards along. Release the beast,
> Lucy's out, it's on! Attempts to extinguish

exuberance, but you're gone. You pounce,
> pitching paws, and prancing like a boxer.
I'm the gong, match marker, stopper, clocker.

Lucy flings into the ring with a facebuster,

> your muscles bulge a moonsault. Pause

> downward dog, then again in Banana Split

> and Peekout scouting your next move. Gong

song, Luchadoras leap into the elevator,

endorphins emanating, meek from misbehaving,
both sit solemnly, silly silent grins, bout breathless.

BIG YELLOW JACK

Big yellow Jack stumbles down from his hairy couch;
he and a novel no one will publish are the only things
    I got from an overpriced New York City MFA.

Jack's the good old wilderness dog of a fellow student
now traveling the world writing for the New York Times,
    while I scoop poop writing my stories and poems

refusing to create more refuse. Jack and me trot on the town,
he throws his weight around, trying to pull me where he wants
    to go, trees of fallen fall-orange leaves and pet store's

rawhide scents blow his nostrils' sneeze. Inside, he spurns
stairs, leather collar slipping over his big head making a fool
    out of me, doormen grabbing sides glee-giggling .

Jack just stands there and stares not budging, too big and old
to drag I know he'll behave, so I tie him up and leave him, ask
    the doormen to keep an eye on him now laying down

licking paws clean. I run up to fetch the younger ones Sally,
Hershey, Lucy bounding up and downstairs with the energy
    that only the young abuse. We elders look on fondly

remembering the spitfire sass we had before New York
had a go at humbling and kicking our ass. But we're not sad,
    we've just learned to work hard and quiet like Darger.

To save our energy, to defend our integrity, we kick out
anyone who disrespects, like Shopsin running his restaurant
    since the 70's for family not just for the money.

The faith that it takes to find your own way in this world
where doubters chirp like maniacal crickets. Some forget,
    the price is high, but if you do your work the rent

gets paid, and you still get to hold on to your soul, bought
and sold so easily, hypocrites one and all. However leashed,
    Jack and me never stop trying to go where we want to.

BERSERK BALLOON BALLET

Big Moe won't give me a break. Boxer bulldozer strut,
    pant, and rush ready for the fight. Rearing up,

anxious screech and cry at the sight of his own kind.
    Excited err—how quick crush craze can fashion

fury. Berserk balloon ballet jeté, the rise and fall of ocean
    waves to my metronome click calm of counterfeit

courage correction. I have to choke him off, swinging
    and spinning in his silver noose. We struggle

until his tongue hangs low to the ground, until his breath
    quickens, slowing him down. Only in exhaustion

can we begin again. As if in a drown-swim, I must first
    render him helpless before I can save him.

I can't push pull him into the pack before he's ready.
    I try my luck with a little cotton ball Cassidy,

she's scared but trusts me. He tries to bat at her head,
    squash her down with his big paw pound.

But I make him sit, turn menace to manners for the first
    time. Curious head turned he watches her walk

and smitten smacks into the trunk of a tree. I chuckle
    and walk on, he prances proud—company.

How like him you are my dear, all teeth and talk,
    all hard-shell iding soft sun yellow yolk.

It took a year of cracking before you let me take the leash
    of our heartstrings link and lead us to brighter things.

TUG OF WAR
For Rusty

What happened to you? Gregarious guy knocking
me aside, running up slippery stairs ebullient, bone

in mouth, hopping on the hairy bed fit for a king,
you allow me in, but not to sleep. Stir morning

wake and all eighty pounds of you bounds down
upon me, sniffing and licking, painful paws digging,

giant head nosing and nudging me to my feet. Big
body barking like a girl, not even a bellow, a shriek.

Pulling me to the park, off leash beseech the squeakiest
ball, so you can feel like you're a crazy killing machine.

Drop for catch, wait until I bend down to scream-plead
your demands into my panged ears. Once you've caught

your kill between big teeth you fake fetch, tricking
any empty hand in your lair into and unwitting game

of Tug of War. You won't let go, after only six years
no more Prospect Park's green and trees. Your solid

stride scarred and clicking from surgery. A clock
making us all more aware of time and how little

of it there is. We are all going grayer, clinging
to anything solid in this world ever-changing.

ZWERGPINSCHER
For Sally

"Bark first, ask questions later," your motto,
modus operandi, hard-wired firing electron.
Cattle prod wielding dwarves at Coney Island
shock. You attack movement, light, and sound,
broken leaves blowing across the bare ground.
You're the general, the street police of Lincoln
Place keeping the neighborhood kids in line,
one nipped heel at a time. Tease and tormenter
you mean no harm—just guarding your small self
unintentionally egging the fight of the big guys
on, then hiding behind my naked legs to escape
the assault. Rabid jackrabbit, jeering jackhammer,
barking bulldozer, Napoleon, circus performer
scaling curves to sit on shoulders. A little ball
of fire curled beneath the comforter while I sleep
keeping me warm. Instigating insect burrowing
within skin, sliding through veins, heart bound.

INVISIBLE TRAMPOLINES

Indiana is unimpressed with Amelia's antics,
bounding around on invisible trampolines,

out of nowhere bursts of energy and whim,
electricity, whenever the moment lighting

strikes her. She's a tiger-striped whirlwind,
a bouncing boxer ready for a fake fight;

she delights at snow banks and sand alike,
children screeching after school or anyone

who "Awwws" her goofy grin. She'll show
them, nub tail wagging a frenetic hummingbird

wiggle, she dances figure eights along cement
cracks and splits. Her comrade Indiana

can't be bothered with this. He's serious,
on a mission looking out for imaginary

assassins, tail down shiver cold, too tough
for the sweater, he growls low when I try

to put it on him. Shark eyes black blink
surveying the scene, a reincarnated army

sergeant running drills along the sidewalk
until Amelia bangs her body into him.

momentarily he lets go and does a little hop
along with her remembering there's more

to life than boxing—there's the moment
and all the dancing spins it can dream.

STELLA

I slept, circle of fire surrounding sheets slit-lit carefully
with knives and gasoline—expensive; I've paid the price
    for anything that ever moved me. I burnt the house

down for the third time, ended up damp, broken boarded—
heart extinguished. You rose, a white wisp of smoke floating
    above the wreckage blown by the wind out of orange

embers and scorched splinters. Bounce-boogied your way
into a beautiful Brownstone up the block. There they drop
    big crumbs, savory sausages, brittle baguettes

on the floor for you to lap up. There they leave papers
to be chewed and shredded to confetti. You make beauty
    out of all the broken things, a party where there

is nothing. What could I offer to a sprightly specter?
I have nothing but charred remains, faded faces, empty
    awkward embraces that echo sounds of wrecking

balls and chainsaws. Freedom! I clank the keys to liberation
from hours spent sleeping, waiting. We're both waking
    to this world, time ticking too precious to keep

wasting. A cloud on a string, you float next to me driving
dogs devilish, flowers and weeds cut through concrete
    cracks reaching out in bloom for you. Crafty

carpenter, dashing doll doctor, you carefully rebuild me.
Stuff arms into shoulder sockets, hammer legs back
    into hip joints. Plug the holes of these damned

eyes that keep leaking. Push your cotton candy head
into my clumsy hands, your paws pull lips from teeth
    to smile. Slowly, you teach me to walk again.

CYNOPHOBIA

For Red Dog

Tough guy strut turned goofy, red dog rant, a fiery
Irishman Celt? Pit bull? Vizsla? Monkey? Snapping
whip wire tail banging baseboards, walls, cracking

knees bend excitement. You on the streets—silly sniff
turns scary amidst other dogs' sneaking around cars,
corners, trees. You're a war veteran always under attack.

Buck-whiny-rear wild stallion screech-sit him down
steady, silence the kill rumbling in his thirsty throat.
We can't live with this Cynophobia, the city streets

are filled with creatures, mirrors, and windows reflecting.
Anxious imaginings–chimera in his own image. Frisson
freak freeze at even amiable approaches of your own kind.

About-face, we start by facing Sammy, Shih 'Izu warrior,
blasé shield uncaring, sits still while you shake a nervous
fit growling till growing calm with exhaustion. Fear turns

to fascination and friendship, you follow the walking mop
bop-bouncing, nearly prancing, provoking play running
hallways jumping kangaroo kidding. Then there's Maggie,

friendly grunting girl next door ignores your frustration
until you calm, cool down, collect yourself. Deep breath,
suck in her perfume and stare at the sexy Shepard-chow

till you're smitten silent. Princess in a tower, you imagine
yourself her Prince savior come to rescue and release her.
We bound down four flights of stairs, you follow her lead

observing everything, carefully trying to imprint your memory
with her movements. Tonight instead of just chasing squirrels
and evading, you'll dream of her, your black-tongued fair maiden.

SEARCHING FOR WHITMAN'S BEARD

Brooklyn's sidewalks are covered with yellow leaves
and squashed stinky Ginko seeds from the "vomit trees."

Another day spent searching for Whitman's beard
on barren streets or a bit of his pen and ink inside me.

Four o' clock on the corner of Washington and Sterling,
they're clanking the metal shutters down at Tom's

Restaurant, no more cherry-lime rickeys and smiling
waiters handing out sugar cookies. The sun is dropping

behind the old buildings; I've already been out walking
four hours—hungry, feet ache, shivering. With icicle fingers

I stroke Maggie, she keeps her eyes on the cars whooshing
by until I stop petting, pocketing my hands for warming.

She flips her nose up, an upside-down possum peering
at me insisting my hurting hands will be warmer scratching

in her tangles of thick black fur. But I am ice, I pity-sing,
no one will read my words, I am nothing for the game

playing. Maggie grunts and groans impatiently back at me.
She pulls to sniff bare trees, soon again come green leaves.

HAPPY NEW YEAR, DOG LADY

Brooklyn is newspaper gray today, the first hour
of snow is a Christmas frolic, but then its knives

in the skin, pinpricks in the eyes. The dogs ignore
until melting flakes tickle their skin beneath the fur

and they shake a shower of melt onto me. My bare
hands redden with cold, the blood pumping, trying

to save my freezing limbs. *Why couldn't I shuffle
paper in midtown with the rest of the animals?*

We begin to slush slip a slick stumble. *Maybe, teach
kids to spell and add Orwell style, 2 + 2= 5?* Ice

seeps into my coat and shoes, toes between. *Why
couldn't I just play the games they wanted me to?*

I drop off the last of the dogs and grumble home.
Huff down Underhill. "Happy New Year, Dog Lady,"

some guy shouts as he passes me. I guess he's seen
me around the pavement pound. I smile and say,

"You too." Laugh and remember to be grateful
for all that's been given and taken away.

ACKNOWLEDGEMENTS

Much gratitude to my poet-mentor Barbara Hamby. I'd also like to thank the poets David Kirby, Bob Holman, Cynthia Hogue, Shelia Lanham, Vijay Seshadri, John Koethe, Maggie Nelson and Monica de la Torre for supporting my work. Thanks to US Poets in Mexico and Prague Summer Program participants and faculty where many of these poems were work-shopped. Thank you Dennis Riley, Melissa Febos, Sini Anderson, Kate Travers, Claudean Wheeler, Nathan Strobel, Holmes Rackleff, Alison Alfandre, and the rest of my Brooklyn and Florida Posse, and my family for always supporting and believing in my "brilliant" ideas. Thanks to my clients, the people and animals of Brooklyn for endless amusement and inspiration.

"Berserk Balloon Ballet" appeared in Work Zine 2009

"Tug of War" appeared in Pyramid 2009

"Powerboat Pit Bull" appeared in Clattery McHenry's Wrestling Anthology 2009

"These Streets Aren't Zagat Rated," "Elephant on Brooklyn Bridge," "The Circus is in Town," "Slope," and "The Burroughs of Brooklyn" appeared in Poets and Artists 2009

"Mexican Dogs" appeared in Pyramid 2010

"St. Francis of 42nd Street" appeared in Dog Fancy 2010

"Searching for Whitman's Beard" appeared in Mipoesias 2010

"Diesel Ghosts" appeared in Shampoo 2010

"Bulls of Pamplona," "Wrestling a Cerberus," and "Death of a Love Junkie" appeared in the anthology "Dogs Singing" (Salmon Poetry 2010)

Made in the USA
Lexington, KY
10 January 2012